THE DIRT

The Miami University Press Poetry Series
General Editor: James Reiss

The Bridge of Sighs, Steve Orlen
People Live, They Have Lives, Hugh Seidman
This Perfect Life, Kate Knapp Johnson
The Dirt, Nance Van Winckel

THE DIRT

Poems
by
NANCE VAN WINCKEL

Miami University Press
Oxford, Ohio

Library of Congress Cataloging-in-Publication Data

Van Winckel, Nance
    The Dirt: poems / by Nance Van Winckel.
        p. cm.— (The Miami University Press poetry series)
    ISBN 1‑881163‑06‑7: $15.95. —ISBN 1‑881163‑07‑5 (pbk.) : $9.95
    I. Title. II. Series.
PS3572.A546D57   1994
811'.54—dc20   93‑38356
                                                              CIP

Printed by Cushing-Malloy, Inc., Ann Arbor, MI.

The paper in this book meets the guidelines
for permanence and durability of the Committee
on Production Guidelines for Book Longevity
of the Council on Library Resources. ∞

Printed in the U.S.A.

9 8 7 6 5 4 3 2 1

ACKNOWLEDGMENTS

Thanks to the editors of the following journals in which these poems first appeared:

THE AMERICAN POETRY REVIEW: "Restaurant with Four Minus One," "Under an Imposter's Hat"

THE ANTIOCH REVIEW: "After Hiking All Day"

ASCENT: "Madame Tussaud," "Snowpeople"

THE CHICAGO REVIEW: "Old Man Watching the Storm"

THE DENVER QUARTERLY: "Please Wake Up," "Wake No One"

GRAND STREET: "Ghost Pig"

THE INDIANA REVIEW: "Double Negative," "Girl with Wood"

THE IOWA REVIEW: "Boy Soprano"

THE NATION: "Good Timing"

THE NEW ENGLAND REVIEW: "Cryonics: Born Again into a Cold Light," "Repercussion," "Two Rains"

THE NEW VIRGINIA REVIEW: "Bodily Love"

THE NORTH AMERICAN REVIEW: "Infidel"

THE PENNSYLVANIA REVIEW: "Two-Room Schoolhouse"

PLOUGHSHARES: "Insemination Tango," "Nicholas by the River"

POETRY NORTHWEST: "All the Livelong Day," "Calvary Baptist Church," "Drill, 1957," "Levitation, "Women Talking in Doorways"

SHENANDOAH: "Ascension, Superimposed," "Fish Unlimited," "Last Time I Saw Them"

The author also wishes to thank the National Endowment for the Arts and the Illinois Arts Council for fellowships and Eastern Washington University for a faculty grant, all of which helped toward the completion of this collection.

CONTENTS

I.

II.

III.

IV.

I.

Must I go to a country not yet seen but as close
as the other side of one's senses?
    I'll sail its rivers. I'll go ashore
und ask about its oldest customs.
I'll speak to women in doorways,
watch them calling home their children.

—Rilke, "Requiem for a Friend"

WOMEN TALKING IN DOORWAYS

She suggests I take the dead down
from my walls. Frame something instead
like a wave that never stops
cresting. This is how our lives
want conducting—taking turns
with advice. A little Ming pot
for that corner? A change,
then an exchange of decor. How
to arrange someone else's quiet,
then to rearrange one's own.

Old ordinary twilights surround us.
Maybe a delicate mist is falling,
or a pennant of moonlight flaps on a roof.
Our voices fade in the distance
of street people who drift past.
Or our voices fall beneath trains
that roar overhead. A face in a window
about to be recognized, blurs. Goes by.

Called for, our children step over the rails,
dauntless, having held off sleep,

having shaken their too-early dreams.
Come home, come now. They dart
among our skirts. The fringe of my shawl
tangles in hers, my child's fingers
in her child's. One day we must
sort among the potted plants, hooked
rugs, our ancestors' faces under glass.
That great uncle, was he yours? Mine?

Under An Imposter's Hat

He who sat on the mule and said sweet goodbyes.
As if the tether between us could be broken
by a toxin, a blindness, a wind.

That one wants the song of his two hands lifted
so their labor goes off in a clever loop.

Were there not so much of me
divvied up in tense anatomies,
I might adopt a likewise feeling.

For years my great aunts fed the mule.
Now he's assumed in my wishes the power
to lie down in his radiant reins.

The old aunts in their wicker rockers
askew on the mountain tops say it's little wonder the gods go
wrong on us.

The mule's halter chokes
but still he goes round.

Under the hands of ancient aunts
February's chiseled through the bone.

The aunts rise at the preparation for light.
They wash and wed
and make themselves among us.

Between them and me, at break-neck speed,
generations have expired—exploded, ignited,

drowned—saving other people's children.

I do not love the one whose feet don't fit the stirrups.

Nor do I expect his death will be a charm
to adjust the winds to my liking.

That one, he's got his heart, if not his eye,
turned toward the last town of the west
where yellow lights twink.

The worldview from muleback,
prepared under a straw hat's brim,
it comes to nothing. It hovers
and descends; it rides the ruts.

I am Sophisticatus Erectus in a folktale
the great aunts of these mountains
a hundred years hence will tell, saying:
	she walked at dusk beneath a big duck
	down here alone from the Northern Province.
	Behind, our slow friend slogged his weight
	and ahead, the mountains
	rocked back at the wind.

DRILL, 1957

If we could angle the sunbeam of the song
through our bent bones, we might sparkle ourselves

out of here. If we could lift our foreheads
from the bricks, our knees from the floor,

we might shut down the claxon, stop its deep
irredeemable ache. How long can we do this

before a real thing happens—this filing out,
this kneeling fast, hands up over our heads.

We know the way to make ourselves sunbeams,
even though the teacher paces behind us,

ordering our heads lower, even though
the cold comes rumbling through the bricks

and through my most secret silent voice,
which can never hit the high notes

sweet enough. This prayerful pose
is a lie. It just makes trouble.

We've seen what they think they're hiding—
the overgrown shadows with the overgrown heads.

They follow us out and huddle just over
our own. We get only someone's word for this.

Patience. They call it a practice
for patience. But who can be sure of a bell

so big? Or figure a real sunbeam: what it was
before it was dust, before it was struck through with light.

LEVITATION

Some nights what we didn't know
couldn't stop us. We'd get ourselves
into the same want for the same thing,

and once, just once, it was for neither
hooch, nor weed, nor poker all night
in a new boy's bed—but only to see

how the other half lived, the other half
of ourselves: stripped of its makeup,
disincarnate without its noisy earrings.

The object was to slough off the bulk
of our skins, as if by chance
some slight thing might come over us.

We lay down the lightest—Doreen—
in the middle; Doreen, whose mother
was finally happy: her daughter safe

in the cellar with girlfriends. The object
was to soften ourselves, and to exhale
through our long, extended fingers.

We put in one from each of our hands,
fingers hooked under her heels,
her thighs, her ribs. And mine

the two fingers held to that hard
black place, back behind the skull.
In a new hush of quietness, she bid us

goodnight, and let her body go
like a concrete block. The object was
to synchronize with the basement's hum,

all the machines in action, all of us
quite still and somehow moving,
circling Doreen in our clicking ions.

We felt the cold filling up the space
beneath her. We were nothing but
a network of little nerves, bent

to the same task. We could never
have dreamed such a pure departure
from the foolishness of our lives,

nor the dark expanse our lungs took in,
or the strange strength that came rushing
from nowhere into our hands.

NOTHING TO DO IN TOWN

but drive to the radio tower
and back. Who could count off
the many nights like this? The tower
was one end of a line, then the forest
beyond: telltale smear of pinesap
on someone's elbow. In the forest
if a boy leaned too hard
against a tree, I might confuse him
with the subtle sway and tilt of what
I thought was tree. Not
his body turning to me, not his back
settling back on rough bark.

       I could be four or five trees away.
       And calling. I could be wrong
       about the drive home, the way
       out of there. Taking his forgiveness,
       I'd have to take the very body
       in which it was offered, the body

that finally stood apart from the tree,
light lifting from the leaves
to find us. The tower kept blinking,
kept backing away. Hadn't we been sent forth
with certain deeds to perform? Which ones?
What were they? Spines pressed to a bed
of pine needles, we tried to call up
a nameless thing from farther back.
High above, heavenly bodies deserted us
taking the heavenly orders with them.

I could be two or three trees away.
I could answer his call,
stand up tree against body again,
and clean pinesap from my elbow.
I could give back forgiveness now—
a new light lowered into old leaves—
and walk out from there. Clock hands
come together like one hand.
Strike the hour. Go home.

LAST TIME I SAW THEM

How they gathered at the end of a pier,
the lake still with its crust of ice
left on. I'd been in love with one

or maybe two of them, boys to whom
that kind of cold meant nothing.
I was in a breath of fog, watching

from someone else's truck
when the boy farthest out
raised his arms over his head.

I wanted to see that ice break.
Never mind other fields old men
spoke of hoeing. I wanted to see

those bodies fall, hear the whacks
on the water. But the truck was already
pulling out—gravel spray and grind of gears—

and looking back, I saw them all still
poised there, still daring, waiting
for someone to make the first move.

IRREDEEMABLE ONE

Late at night I sneak off to the park
to speak with the leader of an ordinary
oddball religion. It's got a mandolin
accompaniment: the man's fingers
in the air, on the tinny strings,
in love with something that can't
bring itself to call itself God.

For no rewards can his children
be made to sing us a hymn.
They kick a dog-shaped balloon
off trees and shrubs. I'm at my distance
from what he says, just beyond
his good arm's reach. Of what use
such innocence? The dog deflating
in the cleft of a tree. The man's lips
part the words, one from another,
how the deity in us is in a sorry
state. Silvery shadows hurry
his talk along and give the park
this shimmer. The park.

The park takes its name
from these birches, which were here
before us. The park is no one's.
And the nothing that's not here
can't be made to come from us, only
through us. As it has. As it always
has. I reopen my window
and climb back in, try to settle the self
that keeps free-falling away
from the others. Now lay us down
to sleep. Let go the breath
that blows through us.

NOTHING IN THE WORLD

Someone I loved twenty years ago had seen three men
rope a fourth man's torso to a tree, then tie his arms and legs
to the rear axle of an Army jeep. He said the three men laughed
when the jeep lurched and couldn't have heard the one scream
that hovered a long time in the branches. The three men
had been of one race, the man at the tree another,
and the man I loved a third—young enough then
to say all this had nothing in the world to do with me,
and believe that. All I knew of loving him I'd known
from the first—our names written on waters preceding us.
Delicate letters in a swirl on top, and underneath,
stumps and rocks to disperse first one moment of us, then
all signs of us. When the man I loved had seen what he'd seen,
he'd grabbed his rifle and run with it up a road
through a country our country had no business being in,
ready, he said, to blast whatever came next over the dirt ruts.
I didn't think I could last much longer—his wife across town
with her makeup in streaks and her dark hair in ruin,
me shoving my body like a huge stone out his door—one month,
then one more, dressing and redressing in layers, everything
beneath us more rock, fissures of bone and blood.
Stepping into the busy midnight parking lot, even then
I'd wanted that life farther away in time and less clear.
I'd wanted to find my car in a hurry and get out of there;

the bread company's last shift was pulling in, late
in loud Chevys, and the other shift pulling out, and I was
in the way, the wrong color and wrong sex. Mufflers dragging,
sparks flying—what was shouted from car windows only stirred
a poison I'd already swallowed, the last overhead crimelight finally
shot out, me circling the same row a fourth time, a fifth, and Hey,
hey sister, that sweet little white ass ain't long for this world.

I WAS CALLED MADELINE
ON THIS SIDE OF THE BLUE WALL

over which the priest has climbed
and ripped his robes, though the rip,
he's sure, isn't one that matters.
He looks down and away, embarrassed
when I offer him my breasts
to kiss, though they were the reason
he'd climbed. He says Hush now,
he's really no one's father, says
he can't be certain which life
has been the greater mistake.

There was a path through autumn
followed more or less. A far off russet
of rye fields, which the good priests
had yet to get to, to turn under.
Any breeze could make a nearby pine
drop its long fragrant needles.
And the monastery, that huge grey stone,
stood open to the sky. But not to me, not
to one who's lit the fire that sweeps
the field with a flame. I have uncovered
and recovered my sinner's breasts,
shaken out my hair in a wonder of wind
full of ash and char. Up
the hill and down. All
my one life I am ashamed.

(Detail: Blue Dot, Top Right of Canvas)

I am not from here. Am without the straight
dark hair of those from this region. High cheeks
in purple shadow. They who remember my time
in their presence will say she tried with music
to sell something through the hills. A thing
compelled by a strict busyness of her hands.
Late in life she sought to save herself
with silence, having loved one then another of us
alternately. Her blue eyes appear at random
among our youth. Her quiet, her timid gait
have been entangled in all that has passed here
since her demise. Her exact name and particular
kindnesses and errors we cannot quite recall,
or recalling, cannot quite describe.

II.

Did you leave behind somewhere
some Thing that's tormented and wants to follow?

—Rilke, "Requiem for a Friend"

We Were Elsewhere Until Dawn

That night after the fire left the ridge
a territory of moonlit embers,
we found two shovels and made ourselves
the patrol. The great nowhere's breezes
sent sparks into orbit around stumps.

> Unfenced, forgotten, an old man's pig
> poked the smoldering mounds of ash.
> Under us, our boot heels in a slow
> melt. Shovels heavy on our shoulders, when

> > down below, called elsewhere in a hurry,
> > firetrucks had to gun their engines and go—
> > behind them a charred summit on which our dark

> > > turned and withdrew
> > > the way a few pale horses once stole
> > > across stone walls, wounded
> > > but not unhappy.

If You Pass a Blue House
You've Gone Too Far

Twelve miles from Phuoc Vinh
    someone told my husband, back
        when his hair was thick and tinged
            red by a strange sun,

how to stay alive
    on a road that went God knows
        where. Once I wanted only his hand
            in my hair—that alone: nothing before,

nothing after. Wheat on either side of the road
    grown so high, we may as well
        have just entered the world. Going
            to someone named Karen's party,

knowing only if we passed a blue house
    we'd gone too far. How long ago was it,
        he'd said, when he knew by heart
            how bamboo grew. Though years

had slipped past what may as well have slipped
    back into the earth. We left the car
        by the road in a gully. Two rows
            of wheat flattened to shape

a suggestion of no one's presence. Always
    the party we'd be lost to, the fist
        of his hand in my hair hanging on,
            bluer and bluer houses rolling by.

ALL THE LIVELONG DAY

All day connected by a black hose to the sky,
    I've been little more than my own
        slow breaths. I shift in my chair
           and some yellow sand shakes loose
               from the crook of my elbow,

so that when your clenched fist starts moving
    toward my face, for a moment I forget
        it's only for the salt there
           I'm supposed to taste. Then
               the lime, and a clear draught

of something that goes down like nothing.
    I'm still wet under all this, still
        the blonde eel in her red sandals.
           We throw the last crust of bread
               over the rail to the barracuda

and sit back, so far back, our hands
    on the table seem too small for us,
        a bad fit. Why should we worry:
           there's always the lucky worm
               at the bottom to revive us.

Maybe the starlight's starting to wear on us.
   This afternoon I'd been swimming right
      out there. I'd forgotten the barracuda
         and was already deep among them
            when what should have mattered

didn't. Up above, the people like us
      in the restaurant were pointing. I'd appeared
         as the bad dream that floats up
            through the good one. But I'd just
               been passing through. The fish

parted, their phony smiles enlarged
      by their teeth. No one wanted
         to take the first bite. So I
            surfaced on down the beach
               where you had a new bottle

and were waiting. We faced down twilight:
      soup and bread and coins on the table,
         then walked out under even more stars,
            through which we are also only passing,
               still a little weak in the knees.

Restaurant with Four Minus One

The end of J's sentence never arrives
without the slow unwinding of its start.
Could we have memorized any more
of the face of the one about to leave
our table in handcuffs? As if to study
the moment harder might fend off
its sad-faced tyrant of shadows. We barely
get beyond his back—tall and broad
and crossed by the two bound wrists.
Three of us still had mussels
in our mouths, mussels that just
lay there cold in too much
tequila. Someplace not far, nor far enough,
from Nogales. Here, swallow, R. said,
why shouldn't it go down? Why
shouldn't the marimba music
come up, cover our inflated infractions?
Someone's eyes, in a melody, held
the purple sky. She was all
he'd dreamed she would be.
We couldn't get past the bad
translation, past our own overdue
unpaid farewell. Ten years—

that's a sentence a man writes
and rewrites on the wall of his cell,
a sentence in a hand grown every day
more sure of and strengthened by
his anger that's a widening crack
in the brick of madness. So did
the dauntless bandidos dance?
The ones whose list of offenses was just
as long, did they keep to their feet
for a last slow song? That time
was only fear's titillating start.
What's truly frightening is still
months, years down the line.

PLEASE WAKE UP

My father wants morning's clouds
blown off in a hurry. Horses' hooves
over the years have made him deaf.
When his poet, Keats, listened
and leaned too long into one bird's song,
he couldn't believe what he heard.
He let the questions fade out
and in, like my father's face
across the hall. He wants me to wake up
and come with him to the races.
He wants to peel off crisp bills
and hand them to the man
who keeps a list of promises,
all their lovely lucky names.

Out my window there's a bird
giving birth in the air: pained
cries, but only small ones.
The old man's dreams, even
the unlucky ones for me,
have finish lines that snap
and shatter quiet like gunfire.

Hands on his knobby knees,
the sun half-risen, he
listens for me as I turn
and moan in my sleep.

WAKE NO ONE

One night while an ocean liner
cut low through the water,
in the aft ballroom a dance troupe
set the stage in motion. White
legs in the floodlights. Applause
from a packed house. Stars
on wires in the wings
awaited their cues,

as the hull took on
more water from a little hole
that grew like the fingernails
of the dead. Beyond belief.
The tapping of tapshoes
and a steady lowering
down. Someone asked
what's the name of this number.

Later, when the ship was
bow first in the sea floor
and the anemone fluttered
like show girls around it,
I was awakened by the birds
at work. They pecked

through the dirt
for the dirt-eating worms.

I spread the clays of earthy
blue, dusty brown. I've
been carving—and it's almost
complete—the birth scene
of a foreign nation. With
God's hand, shrivelled,
cloud-like, and barely
distinguishable, above it.

I'm Going Out Walking, She Said

And her field was cheatgrass
frosted. Little cupboards in the wall
into which she'd quickly stashed
the dried arrangement she'd been
making: thistle, statice, vetch. *Click,*
and the cupboards closed.

On our porchstep a bottle of milk
had sat too long—inside it,
a slow-motion chaos rearranged
by yellow cuneiform ciphers. Our meadow
was sunstruck. Against it she looked lovely
as my middle-aged sister, moreso
than in pictures which pressed her childhood
inside a neatly trimmed pixie hairdo.

Now she tied a flowered scarf, her
babushka, in a careless knot, and I thought
perhaps as she walked she heard
a line from a poem, and, like a leaf
in her hair, might look at it briefly
before brushing it away, saying it was
nothing, nothing really. For a while

she seemed to walk in a stillness,
though the black branches were blown back.

I had given her shoulders
a massage in my dream,
then phoned her in as a missing person.
Earlier from hers, she'd had
only those four words to say.

Three Wives Weeping

Their tears are not the same,
though each had been a wife once
to this man in his urn now

beneath the wreaths
and the too-red roses. The wives'
tears flow in distinct trails

the jagged, the straight, the wildly
curving—though they cry
in the one way of many

exhausted sadnesses.
Outside, evening plummets
down its hazy hues of dusk,

and on one side of one mountain,
colorful lights flicker. Just so
in their runs of eyepaint, smudged rouge,

the weepers' faces confuse us
with a grief that seems a grief
inverted—clowned and clouded

by the rigors of mourning. Especially
the one in the middle who is
my mother, who takes the hands

of the other two. None among
their sobbing triumverate will say
the urn is hers to have, now that

this sudden flare of anti-mourning
has snagged them, briefly, from eye
to eye. Passed on: a life that passed

through theirs, as they might pass
a familiar mountain at dusk.
Or as the boy in the foyer catches

my eye. Having come to shut
the door on the sanctuary, he is far
beyond us with what else he's doing:

slow chords struck hard
on a guitar sunk low in his arms,
though there is no guitar.

Then I watch from the mountain's foot
as three widows take three separate
switchback routes to the summit,

all the while the foretold front
moving in, hesitant as a long
withdrawn breath over the ridge

Lights along the roadside flicker,
and quit. Then an outright darkness.
Through the cloud-level, up and

out, and with perhaps only a slight
tightening of hands on the wheels,
the women go on pursuing their trails

to the top, where a man's ash may be
loosed upon the sky, until the clouds,
seeded, drop their weight of rain.

INSEMINATION TANGO

A man in the south of France flaps his elbows
and dances with a female crane, who is
the last of the Black-tails. He hoots
and coos, and she lowers her long
delicate neck. Yesterday the man had sunned
and swum amid a swarm of nude swimmers
in the Riviera's cloudy waters, so that now
his skin shines pink, his bald spot
darkened. He lifts his arms, and the bird
lifts her wings. He struts, high-stepping
across the pen in which she's lived her whole
life, and has come to allow this display
of a man's possible desire. The flutter
of black tail feathers, raised: her iridescent
acquiescence. That low sweeping squawk:
her answer of longing. And though the man's
response is silly, strange, and sadly
wrong, it will do to stir her enough—so that
whatever he's hiding, whatever he's holding
in that clenched flailing fist like a secret
kept too long alone, she can finally let him
let go—now that she's ready to stand still
and take whatever this love is he's giving.

FRIENDS IN THEIR HELICOPTER CIRCLING

Not far from the given place
and close enough to the given time,
I was out gathering the ripe morels
in dense woods. Startled from my servitude
by the rain's. —And by the whirl overhead.
My friends' gaze stayed hidden
in the pines' ever widening skirts,
though our affection for their airs
trembled in a rotorized mist.

My bag was loaded deep with spores
of barely digested pasts. And by my feet
the mistake I'd picked up last: Mr. slimy
slug, and where in the world were his eyes?
I saw his slime feelers extend
and retract. They navigated an idea
of earth. But no clue about
the sky. As my friends zinged it,
the air, a quick goodbye meant for me.

They were off to count the gone and
going elk. Farewell. Off to cold pastures
farther north, where among census takers
those first pure solitudes began.

And bye to the big blades blowing past,
I stepped into the clearing. So long,
we waved upwards and downwards—until
at the designated spot between many moving
hands, our waves were met upon the air.

III.

I'll observe how, through the ancient work
of fields, they enter the landscape.

—Rilke, "Requiem for a Friend"

SNOWPEOPLE

Drippety-drip, drip
for too many days of unexpected sun
shrinks our family to painful heaps
in the yard, dirty distortions
of our old selves. What protection
did we have, anyway, from the warm light
that tries to measure too much
against itself? All that's left
is to speak bravely and softly
of family matters, even while big blackbirds
shriek and leap from our sagging shoulders.

As snow crystals go, so go
we all. Our father says this. He aims
to be instructive about the urgency
of this final stand-off with the light.
Little brother, the one we call Toad,
won't stop repeating it, as if this makes him
happy. Happy little doomed Toad—
his voice slowing like an old victrola's.

My sister just goes on about experiments,
what could be performed on us all—if we'd only
throw off our white slumps and think kindly

of travel in sudden underground streams.
But mother is suspicious and keeps her good eye—
red potato—on that circle of soil she's about
to penetrate, about to take to herself alone.
She'd like to thank the children who made her,
who gave her those breasts like rockets,
which droop now, leaving cold flares on her belly.

We don't pretend to speak of what we long for most:
to share a chill again, a bright frigid blast,
or any of the obscure goings on
high up in the cold latitudes. Besides,
it's too late. Our malaise has left us
ugly. We've popped our stone buttons,
sent our branch-arms soaring on the various
winds. And only today birds came and pecked
the last raisins of our smiles,
so that when the children rush out
they can't stand to look at us.
They turn to begin their chores: lugging
manure, chopping up sod for a garden.

INFIDEL

Spring and fall the groundhog goes everywhere
we go, trailing his rank odor
of hard labor beneath the green level.
He listens for our big steps, sudden
across his long night tunnels: spirits
of porchlight, deities of dense underbrush.
Damp, subtle evenings he feasts
on our windfall apples, keeps our plastic cast-offs
as relics for his back room, the rear annex.

All winter he wakes to our scraping
and shoveling, our little ways out
to the barn, past the small hole
through which he's barely breathing,
through which he hears us as in a dream:
the aimless wandering ones
in thick robes and blue hats, busy
at their senseless tasks, calling him
back into the high light world.

BODILY LOVE

The back bends back. What
of pleasure can a girl learn
alone in a bed? Secrets
the body shimmies loose
then fills by itself.

The back bends forward, and this
means work: a man on a roof
hammering shingles; a woman inside
long gone in a poem all day. Where's
the virtue they long for? The mind
off in a word, the eye on a hip,
and the heart. . . the heart stalling.

The long guilty trail of embarrassing
sunlight, and the back unbends.
Long nails gone askew. Our teachers
told us to look away from the tough eye
of desire; then something wholly better
and not of the body would set us trembling.

We rise from our work, hammers
heavy in our hands. We shake
the knots of the body as if
to untangle them. We stand
and straighten our backs
as if we're faultless, as if we're
spokes on which the twilight reels.

Nicholas by the River

Two heaps of clothes by an old stump,
and Nicholas neck-deep in that water
too cold for our own good. Shimmering
when he said he wasn't sure but thought
maybe it was a man he wanted,
though I was what he had
under his hands in that blue current—
darker and rougher in the middle
over the deep spots. Nearly the end
of eighteen, and too late in August not
to expect even that which I'd been denied.

Upriver a couple hundred yards
an old man dropped his hook & sinker
and was already watching it drift away
when he saw us—our pair of heads
like two white rocks at the river's edge.
So nothing need have gone much
further. No one need have groped
in the furious currents, or the lovely lazy fish
have come to harm in our close proximity.

And I need not have taken my friend
around behind the craggy jut of rocks

and bent over him as he lay back
shivering in the sun. Maybe it was
not even necessary for him to moan a little
and turn me from him, bend me forward,
head down, hair dragging the water,
so he could enter me the only way
he knew, saying sorry sorry sorry.

AFTER HIKING ALL DAY

Half-gone myself under bad wine
and blues guitars, I helped someone up
off the floor. So much smoke in song
could fill us back then too full. The man
fell again. I didn't know yet
he'd one day be my husband. The place
reeling in pools of light in Denver's
foothills. Get up, I said. Get
up. Hours before, stumbling down
half-made trails, knee-deep
in yellow grasses, I'd lost myself on a ridge.
The someone who sang down in the valley
about its lonesomeness made it all
more lonesome. That was before a bass player
plugged himself in, took the beat
even deeper. We tried to hum along
but failed. We were both laid low.
Two stones that skipped three, four,
five times across a blue lake
and fell.

PATCH LAKE, GHOST TOWN

On its edge—Russian olives, tipped, blighted,
wrung out. Going nowhere with a dusk circling
on far flung wings. Slow flap, flap—then
the sudden hush and lunge of insects below.

What we were doing there you couldn't say.
Stepping from scrub oaks and storefront crumblings,
I'd seen a moon too heavy for its sky: pinned
like a huge weight over the lake's little water.

I sat ashore on a stump. You weren't sure how
long we'd be staying, or how long you'd be off
in that boat. To fix either of us there is a slow stoop,
a shard of memory retrieved: first the long

jaw, then its face, loosened from a landscape
like a splinter from the flesh. So that when your
white oars flashed, you rowed a coming and a going,
a rising and falling of many long-gone darknesses.

Two Rains

falling, exhausted, through American airspace.
From cliff rocks we saw the parti-colored zigzag
   of bathers' blankets down the beach.
We hadn't the heart to climb lower
   to where yet another load of rain
was about to fall—there, on two lovers who still
   had their toes in the tide.
While glint of sea with the wide sun
   backing off, as it had before
and would again. We could tell
   as the lovers touched and stepped
away from touching, they were new
   to each other. Though from where
we stood, certain particulars blurred out:
   insignia of sun on a body,
etched—seen when a strap falls back.

• • •

Saying nothing, we just drove away
from another crisis of family: some punk
    at a loved one's door, pockets
full of pills and his hands out for money,
    and she, down as she was at the end
of her rope. And us as we were driving
    too far in a grey plume of smoke.
Your face in its exact delineations of trouble
    was a blue sheen on the windshield.
Though it was for a day of no trouble
    we'd travelled, tunnelled miles
through one storm already and climbed the sharp rocks
    to put those lavender hills behind us.
Down there the lovers stepped back from the water
    and took each other roughly—a mesh
of indiscernible arms. And then our brief surprise
    when the rain we hadn't wanted to touch us
did, and us feeling none the worse for it.

OLD MAN WATCHING THE STORM

I turn a hundred ways toward a few plain objects
which turn from me. Forty-one days of drought,
then this. I pull the tarp over the rabbits' cages,
roll up windows. My time and the time of objects
split. Across the hedgerow my neighbor sits
amid the thousand empty flower pots of his garage,
amid the hoes and traps, the door signs and shovels
In his chair, through black light, the body that is
and isn't there. I call the sheep in, the dogs
home. Old man in his cone of light, his juncture
of past and future. Tousled hair in tousled shadow.
Is dominates. Until the storm comes. I pass
and he waves his slow wave. The animals bark back
at the thunder. Against the artifice of my lawn
the peonies, even swelled as they are with ants,
bend and shake loose. Old man with his hand
in the air. He holds it out for the first big drops.

When the second heart attack came, he'd been driving
down South Hill Boulevard. Lost on his way
to finding the brake with his foot. Steep descent.
Wild pulsing of light that thuds to a stop.
Three lanes of oncoming traffic crossed

and crossed again. Every ambulance in town
rushing back into the horizon of events.
The hand falls. I try to close the doors
on the hayloft. I pull. They fly back.

In one of his beer signs two men in a boat
row endlessly around a clock on a lake.
They cast and pull up the same bass forever,
the bass that comes up and hangs in the sky.
Old man takes the storm in his hands, time
all around at its perfect stopping place,
the big-mouthed fish about to either speak
or fly away, or fall finally into the net.

GOOD TIMING

On a ridge a wild horse is running
and down below, a young girl timing him—
from one pine to another. Fingers
wrapped around her wrist, she's counting
her heartbeats. Fingers placed
to the pulse as if to cover
a tightly held secret. The way
the horse's legs throw the sky
into motion. Should she tell
her brothers about him? The fingers
lift, but the beating hooves go on.

Such counting runs a secret down
like a clock. Two-bit lessons in kissing
she's learned in the movies. Say the kiss
of 1937. And no one to practice on
but the blue shadows of the hedgerow.
The dark horse, he listens and runs, listens
and runs. Had someone off camera
been timing the two mouths' shared
exchange of air? Their audience
more breathless than any other?
Unwrap the fingers. Halt the stream

of numbers. Let the horse return now
into the far, unobservable trees.

Under her brothers' new rope
the horse is helpless. He runs away
with himself. All through autumn
he deepens a path at the very edge
of the corral. The man she'll finally kiss
hasn't seen the movie. Come January,
he isn't sure what to do: stranded
in her father's porchlight, all her warmth
coming at him in all that cold.

The horse, he's a tough one to figure.
He bucks off the rider, then
the saddle. How to know if he'll ever
stop, if she'll one day get her hand
through those reins. He pulls loose
from the tether and goes round.

GHOST PIG

He has turned his back on the red pullets
pecking at a fallen fenceline. Grey pig
with white rings around his eyes. He steps
onto a nothing little gravel street
that'll soon veer off for the freeway.
I'd come to gather huckleberries
till the hour greyed up. So much dust, grit,
I left behind. A few wings were flapping
but the garbage-fed gulls were too full
to fly. The pig's tail was the last thing
to disappear from the road: flashed
like an inked question mark against the low
brambles. Once there was water down there,
sure, across the road, around on the other
side, way over and much farther back.

GIRL WITH WOOD

To fill up the bin, four more trips.
Radio man saying weather isn't anymore
the same. Father feeling this front
back behind his knees. He winds the scarf up
around my neck, and my mouth mumbling
its too much nothing gets quiet. Quiet
but for the one, two, three
clatter of oak against my chest. Four,
five, six—I'm a tower about to tumble
to rubble. Rumble of logs down stone steps.

Father loads me up again. Feel the height
of someone tall in my boots. Steady, steady
under a small moment's presence. Ice fog
moving in around us, and around two quail
on the roof, scratching to waste time
against the gutters. Here, over the top
log, what's to see? Old dog-eyes
under the porch, red between the slats.
Head for those. He's got his bone-mine
down there. He opens a hole, eats.

Help, Help!

My cries for help dotted every *i* of the fenceposts.
I was the fool standing in the hayfeeder,

as the ram three times my weight circled, head down,
his low foghorned baah cutting the heat between us.

Not another human soul in earshot. So after a while
I just quit calling. I tried kindness and reason,

more foolhardiness aimed at the dumb animals.
All the world who knew me, who might be

stirred by my loud bleating were busy loving
each other: feeding, bandaging, washing,

wounding, bandaging—busy answering other calls.
While the ewes nibbled hay at my ankles, confused

by my red shoes. For a moment the fool in the feeder
isn't funny, alone unto herself as a quality of love

long observed in this corral nears extinction.
Certain callouses on my palms—so what?

The ewes *all* belonged to the ram, which was
the point he'd been trying to make, pawing the dirt

three times, lowering his head, and coming at me
so fast I had to turn foolish and jump in here

where even the old yellow hay has been eaten.
So that now the feeder is empty. Except for me,

a woman between the slats with the sun going down,
the time for serious wooing coming on, and the point
clear enough at last that she's bound to finally get it.

IV.

Tell me—must I travel?
Did you leave behind somewhere
some Thing that's tormented and wants to follow?
Must I go to a country not yet seen but as close
as the other side of one's senses?
I'll sail its rivers. I'll go ashore
and ask about its oldest customs.
I'll speak to women in doorways,
watch them calling home their children.
I'll observe how, through the ancient work
of fields, they enter the landscape. I'll ask
for an audience with their king; I'll bribe the priests
to let me stand before the most powerful statues
in their temple, and then to leave me there,
shutting the gates behind them.

—Rilke, "Requiem for a Friend"

CRYONICS: BORN AGAIN INTO A COLD LIGHT

So now they would bulldoze me out of this sleep
the same way they bulldozed me in.
    They snapped on my headgear, sliced
    a gravel pit open beneath me.

They want to swoop the earth
with their frozen little dolls,
    who like me are everywhere
    and nowhere.

The lid lifts, and I'm sliding forward
one more time, careening down the metal chute,
    the ionized tunnel through which
    my life reconnects to theirs.

My face buoys on frozen casket light.
I give back the dazed expression I was issued.
    They turn me over, turn me up,
    turn me on.

I was living in a kind of double-time,
bygones and bygones of dubious saxophones,
    the sweeping brush across the snare,
    until the needles started in on my toes.

They who loved to stop the pump once,
or maybe twice, just to start it up again,
        now they watch it kick in;
        they watch the sparks fly.

I've been delayed by the dream of a white leaf
suspended on chill air. Finally it falls—
        down and down, while the earth's
        deep strata keep drifting.

Into their strange little smear of light
my wandering memory of wondering faces
        stops: here's the touch, the smile
        to unwind my brief era of silence,

even as in Siberia an older age of ice cracks.
That's when a wooly mammoth lurches, stands,
        and shakes out his snowy coat. That's when
        his thousand-year-old lice start hopping.

ASCENSION, SUPERIMPOSED

(Flea market; Richmond, Illinois)

Under the noon sun we all stop
where Christ on his cross droops
from his nailed hands. Just as

the holy ornament shown, in the end
suffering might propel us through
and out the body. But step an inch

to either side, see the face in the relic
in ascent. Who among us would touch
the rusty light sockets by his feet?

We sense his sheer drop from the cross
to us, and keep quiet. Angels
with full shopping bags. The awful sums

he could, he should, exact from us,
the poor and the sad who can't
but must afford him. Home then

to our table of trophies. Will he
somehow survive the journey? Are all
the stories in this one world about it?

Boy Soprano

If I keep my eyes on their window
the saints who've saved me before
might save me again. If I let the voice
come up, it moves my head to one side
and folds its long hand
into my own two small ones.

Spun from glass and an early angle
of sunlight, blue robes make the men
holy, make them saints forever.

I sing what I'm told to sing—
so the congregation will confess
a slightly larger fraction
of their low abiding love, a fraction
for the fraction they've been given.

Sometimes when I open my hands
the singing does two things at once:
it leaves me and it stays behind.
It goes out, and with its bony fingers
touches shoulders and hats in the aisles.

Then it's not like the dark lonely thing
that leaves me and stays in the night,
sometimes leading me so far, I wake
uncertain of the way back, unsure from what
I've been separated for good.

I have to sit up and open my mouth.
Just to be sure. I start the song,
and there it is to finish itself.

It wakes my brothers down the hall.
Their lights come snapping on
and they appear, round my bed—
me with the voice pumping its good
Welsh hymn, and the little ones
rubbing their eyes—sung loose
from one dream to another.

I fold my hands tighter
and take the song higher.
I let my robes fall back, fall
away, until I am myself uncovered,

the befuddled infant, the 14 years
that add up to nothing.

How long can it last?
I ask everyone. If I dare
to think of a certain girl's hand
on my shoulder, and then
my shoulder laid bare, will
something begin to break?

No one answers, except to say
it *will* break, and it will leave me.
And I'm just to go on
as if what must happen
means no more than an old window
falling in, so many blue and holy eyes
cast down, shattered.

Calvary Baptist Church, 1957

If they'd give her the crayon she'd show them
a few things about red, not like the red fib
of the minister's carnation. But the red to keep
a child still, to make a long-necked pony where once
there was nothing. Let him *out*, shouts the minister.
The green and quiet hills are calling.

Or with yellow she could color down the sides
of the church bulletin, draw her pointy stars
around the prayers, beginning with a few
for the dead Miss Bess. Now whose wild
heel and toe will set itself against the hymns
and make the saints in the windows shiver?

And when she's been good, they let go of the big
purple. Then she gets it in her fist,
the thick dark one. And just in time, just as
everyone leans forward to hear what the minister
really means about the life after life,
what he's trying to say but can't

to the boy he lifts over the black tub
and pushes under. Then she stops her stick people
dead in their tracks, and hurries along
the new creature, the one who moves so slowly
on wobbly purple legs, while that boy, poor thing,
is still down there, still coughing up bubbles.

Two-Room Schoolhouse

(Mt. Vernon, Virginia, 1958)

When I'm bad I'm given ten white pages.
If I make my letters tall, I can make them
toe the lines. I can plant a row of t's,
then another, crossing and recrossing
every black stunted stem along the way.

Often we work alone like this, grades 1-3.
From the loft upstairs, our teacher's a dream
who climbs down to us. The devil's wind
bangs on the window, and she steps down.
Say I don't remember something right,
I get to sit quiet at my desk until I do.

Then I think of the big door up the road,
the bad wind banging there too, long ago.
And the old father in his wooden teeth
getting up to answer. I watch him disappear,
though the teeth remain—two rows
of splinters on a glass shelf.

Teacher's slow on the rungs, pausing
to remind us that anyone who works hard
can plant himself deep into history, send out
taproots of dull intervening incidents.
We say the lesson back, and back again,
until the white wig falls off
and we forget our good manners—
our laughter too loud at the school play.

And who's laughing loudest, whose little teeth
clattering towards a table's edge,
then winding down to just that smile
without its face? I've been trying
to remember this right, the wrong I did,
having sat here quietly all morning.

DOUBLE NEGATIVE

The amoeba I'd only moments before
seen floating under glass, and ha!—
your face just as predictable
against the hallway windows.
Outside, the rain. . . the rain steady.

I descend slowly, me in my splint
of practiced speech. And because
you knew where I'd be, you'd be waiting.

The stink of laboratory life
all around us. Once in a panic
I stuck my hand in a jar of insects
to save from contamination my last
control bee. No one there didn't not
see this, when I pulled out my hand
with its six stings—and saved nothing.

I carried down a week's worth
of anger, so if there were
a stair railing to hang on to, I did.

You were just back from the war
and married, taking a step

away from the window to lift
a book off the top of my stack.

Down from the well lit lab,
the tall yucca with its bent spine,
to this: students out the doors
in a hurry, blur of glasses
and raincoats. Could any of us forgive
the stings that redeem nothing?

Holding hard to that rail, my hand
in its white bandages, I wanted
too much at once: for there
to be rain, for you to take your place
against the wet glass. And for
the rain to stop, to stop us.
For your marriage to take you back.
For the tall windows to stand behind
something just as wild and wet
and disastrously wonderful as your face,
but that was not your face.

Repercussion

(Laramie, Wyoming, 1976, Rodeo Days)

Meg and I were with two guys we thought
we could someday love and on our way
to a girlie show. *You, you lovebirds,*
you can park your horses here was the barker's
cry along a pleasure street. The girl inside
walked across five tables to get to ours.
Her cunt was a mouth she fingered open
before the four of us, who may as well
have been doctors looking for blisters
in her throat. *Clearly she wanted*
to vex us, Meg said to me. *Vex, hex, sex,*
said her lover, fully drunk on her arm
in the alley; *she was getting off*
on the reper-fucking-cussions of her art.

Which took us back then, Meg & me, to our girl faces
in the joint's half-light, where we tried not to look
or look away. Like this was part of the grand errand
toward some ultimate freedom that began
as a clear line of vision up the far curve
of our own insides—all we had never seen
out of the private trust, smoke-lit and

music-laden in the public hoots of the world—
that mouth standing open for the huge delivery
of a long-terrified, horrified shout. Seething
and writhing farther up in the dark, what might
the word have been, had it ever come out?

A Dozen Identical Gowns
On the Dancefloor

There in my blonde French twist,
I meant to be found by someone
who kept keys to the kingdom
of ease. Nevermind he was twice
my age. Up front, on stage a big
performance number: dancers
whose feather fans
expanded the whole idea
of diamonds. Already I had the sense
I'd never again wear the blue gown,
cut low, or dance that way,
keeping the keys in the man's pocket
jingling. The showgirls we watched
were meant to be seen from a ceiling—
each face an oval smudge
bending its jeweled headdress
toward one, then another
geometrical ardor. Looking down at his ten
ancient knuckles, for a moment I made
that old skin peel back to reveal hands
in a frenzy of young desire—not

those trembling careful hands
counting out chips I could place
on whatever bets I chose, just
so long as they were the red numbers,
only the red ones *please,* whirling
in a blur down the belly of the wheel
the way my luck would have it.

My Brother Picked Me Up

He shut down the boat and we lay back
on a stack of rotting life vests. The egret
was a lavender shadow circling, pulling
at the water—one way, then another.

From the center of the lake we could see
a figure looming on shore: our father
whom I was to know as stepfather
but could only hear as step farther,

that man alone and perpendicular
to the dock. He rattled an empty
bait pail. My brother had picked me up
past him. He'd lifted me and lifted

the gravel out of a cut on my knee,
sopped at the thin red trail down my leg,
and carried me past my mother
who was not his mother, though once

she'd shown him her garden of tiny pea blossoms
and fat fists of cabbages that were nothing
he'd ever seen. He picked me up—high
on the tanned scaffold of his shoulders

and past the one brief summer he was
my brother, before he was flown back
to a state and a mother that existed
on another side of an earth much like

our own, though first he had to fly
across the snowy egret's path. First
the sun-stroked clouds had to part for him
like a river of blood.

FISH UNLIMITED

So I asked my father how many more—
those mackerel that just kept coming,
flapping across our feet, my arms
tiring fast from reeling them in.
We'd hit a school of them, and everyone
was pulling them on board, all our friends
and our parents' friends, and their friends,
and everywhere those dying fish flopping.

The sun strung itself higher, harder,
a wire angle bent through the eye.
Still we yanked more in. No matter
the slippery deck, the heavy rods.
No matter the little minnows
all awiggle. We had only to reel
and reel, ankle deep in blood, bodies
flapping, splayed mouths agape.

We were laughing. The mackerel were so
silver, so cool against our legs. *Holy,*
someone said of them, words drifting
back to us on the oceanic wind. There was
this one time of too much money. Too many
noisy flags on the bow. We thought given
enough speed, our boat might outrun
its own huge white wake.

RUBES

My father with his hand in a man's mouth,
    kneeling over a plaid-suited body
        on a street in New York City.
We had just bought warm chestnuts from a vendor
    and given our change to a legless man
        who wheeled by us on a pine plank,
and we'd walked a ways north when the next event
    happened. Which was a seizure, a thing
        my father recognized. The man moaned
and appeared to throw himself to the sidewalk.
    His eyes in a rush to release the city's
        last window, last light. His head
banged back. Then my father called for a stick,
    a pen. Then my mother fumbled a while
        in her purse. Until the hand—that
which had come at us, palm against our cheeks
    in little blows for years—until that hand
        went into a stranger's mouth.
And it stayed. People glancing and passing;
    someone's two legs kicking. Sisters, mother,
        standing, staring in a stupor.
And the hand where it was until the man
    was ready to speak, his eyes hard and straight
        on the stranger who was my father,
and though the words the man said were clear
    and beautiful against the chill November air,
        there wasn't one we knew, coming
            as they did from some faraway nation.

MADAME TUSSAUD

Visitors' feet on the magic wires
make my glass doors part. Goodbye
and goodbye. My hand's on a motor
and it waves. If the world's traffic
honks, I bid them back to it. Though
some days when the wind turns hard,
turns cold, I don't. My hand waves
in the dark at no one.

Then I open the drawers of dreams
and dip into my stock of old eyes.
With long thin needles I sew hair
into skulls. There's a face to stretch taut
around every right or wrong-headed scheme
and poses to perfect a thousand
thousand passions. I pour beeswax
into molds and pop out assorted faces

of friends and fools: my patroness
the Princess, Robespierre, and Marat
murdered in his slipper bath. I drift
so far back in my long past tense that when
the voice of la Guillotine calls,
I bend down and pick up the heads.
I rinse loose the blood and efface
a lifetime of memory into one hard look.

My heads cook. They bake all day,
while I return through the vaulted rooms
of the many selves, splintered off here
and here, repositories for what cannot
be revived: all the lovely motions
made toward loss. Oh my liege, my
Louis, how often will my own head
roll free of its body and stare

back at it for those moments, unafraid?
How often will I rise and walk out
the Reign of Terror's other door?
I put a plum in a pie for Jack Horner.
I shine the little lusters of love
in his eyes, rub a spot of grime
off the cheek of a young country's father.
My hand's on a motor and it waves.

Nance Van Winckel received the Society of Midland Authors Award for her first collection of poems, **Bad Girl, with Hawk** (University of Illinois Press, 1988). She is also the recipient of a National Endowment for the Arts Fellowship in Poetry, and her poems have appeared in **The American Poetry Review, The Nation, The Georgia Review, Poetry Northwest, Shenandoah, Ploughshares, The North American Review,** and other journals. Her first collection of short stories, **Limited Lifetime Warranty,** is available from the University of Missouri Press. She is the current director of the M.F.A. Program at Eastern Washington University and editor of **Willow Springs.**